This Is My Book

My name is _____

_____

My cat is called _____

_____

For David Ford

First published 1998 in *The Necessary Cat* by Walker Books Ltd
87 Vauxhall Walk, London SE11 5HJ

This edition published 2002

10 9 8 7 6 5 4 3 2 1

"The Lion" and "The Tiger" from *Cautionary Verses* © Hilaire Belloc;
reprinted by permission of The Peters Fraser and Dunlop Group Ltd
on behalf of the Estate of Hilaire Belloc

A variety of typefaces has been used in this book,
with handlettering by Annabelle Davis

Printed in Hong Kong

British Library Cataloguing in Publication Data:
a catalogue record for this book is available
from the British Library

ISBN 0-7445-9432-4

THE CURIOUS CAT

*A Celebration of Cats in Pictures,
Stories & Rhymes*

NICOLA BAYLEY

WALKER BOOKS
AND SUBSIDIARIES
LONDON · BOSTON · SYDNEY

Contents

Cat Scraps

GATÃO
PUSS IN BOOTS
VINHO VERDE
Região Demarcada
BRANCO 75CL

PRODUCT OF PORTUGAL

Chocolat POULAIN
Goûtez & Comparez

8_ Le Chat Botté

I HAVE MADE A HASH OF THINGS!

15 भारत
INDIA

6

SOMETHING ON MY MIND

Copyright 1905
Rotary Photo

Mackintosh's
Nurseryland
Toffee de Luxe

MARY
CONTRARY

tosh's
ryland
e Luxe

PUSS IN
BOOTS

Mac
Nu
Tof

TEA TIME

Уссурийскій Тигръ ПОЧТА СССР 25 КОП

THREE CATS
REG'D TRADE MARK
Manufactured by Spruce
MADE IN ENGLAND

Kitty
PLAYING
BALL

WIND UP

串國製造
MADE IN CHINA

"Got Sumthin."

THE YOUNG PRACTITIONER

the fight begins when

you pull the strings

cat marionette

wind-up cat

prrr rrr rrr

CATS IN THE TOY CUPBOARD

if you know how, you can make this cat crumple

Three Little Kittens

THE NEW TIDDLYWINK GAME

6 3 2 4 1 5

what fun — kitty tiddlywinks!

this tin cat has lost his key!

pull the string and pussy chases the mouse

articulated cat

10

finger
puppet

cats to cuddle

tiny
jigsaw
cat

a cat
to clutch

doll's
house cats

hand
puppets

shake the
mouse and
tease the cat

press my back to make me *miaow*

an old
board game,
with tiny
china cat and
mouse pieces
on a merry
chase

The New Game
"POUNCE"
FOR TWO PLAYERS

PUBLISHED BY
J. JAQUES & SON, LONDON

11

Bella Counts to Ten

1 one
hot radiator

2 two
strong brushes

3 three
warm lights

4 four
willing laps

5 five
favourite plants

6 six
different dishes

7 seven
scratching books

8 eight
fat mice

9 nine
tangly balls

10 ten
small birds

Cats Can Be...

Alien

Bashful

Cunning

Dim

Enormous

Foolish

Glorious

Hairy

Idle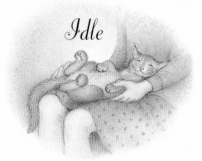

Jolly

Kindly

Lean

Magical

Naughty

Obstinate

Proud

Quiet

Ridiculous

Silly

Talented

Unfortunate

Valuable

Worrying

Xenophobic

Yowling

Zealous

19

Exotic Cats

1 Japanese Bobtail

2 Sphynx

3 Egyptian Mau

4 Turkish Van

5 Birman

6 Devon Rex

7 Scottish Fold

8 Odd-eyed Angora

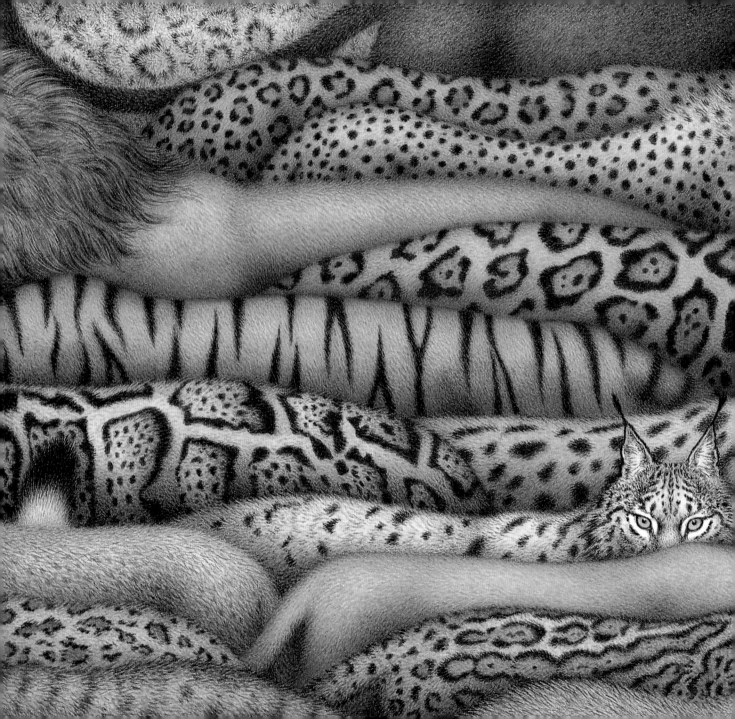

Lion

Tiger

Panther

Clouded Leopard

Wild
C A T S

Snow Leopard

Caracal

Jaguar

Leopard

Cheetah

Lynx

Bobcat

Ocelot

Serval

Margay

Wild Cat

Sand Cat

23

The composer Champfleury claimed to hear 63 separate notes in a cat's mew.

A cat can have as many as 120,000 hairs per square inch.

The first exhibition of cats took place at Crystal Palace in London in 1871.

Did You Know That...?

Tiddles, the ladies' room cat at Paddington Station, London, weighed 32 lbs and had his own refrigerator.

No two tigers have the same markings.

"The Cat & Fiddle", a popular name for English pubs, was carelessly borrowed from the French for "The Faithful Cat", which is *Le Chat Fidèle*.

Of all cat breeds, only the cheetah cannot retract its claws.

Cheshire cheeses were commonly moulded into the shape of a grinning cat.

The Fishing Cat, *Felis viverrina*, has partially webbed feet.

The tiglon, a hybrid of a lion and a tiger, is bred only in captivity.

White cats are very often deaf. ᖾ

When a cat is frightened, it sweats through its feet. ᖾ

All white tigers of Rewa are descended from Mohan, who died aged 19, leaving 114 white descendants with ice-blue eyes. ᖾ

It was once thought that the dung and urine of a cat could cure baldness. ᖾ

The black tuft on a lion's tail conceals a claw or spur. ᖾ

Motherly cats will suckle otter pups. ᖾ

A bottle foster mother comes in handy for an orphaned kitten. ᖾ

The Savoy Hotel in London employs Kaspar, a wooden cat in dinner dress, to be the fourteenth guest for parties of thirteen – thus avoiding bad luck! ᖾ

The paws of *Felis bieti*, the Chinese Desert Cat, are very hairy to protect them from the hot sand. ᖾ

The author's cat loves melon and beetroot. ᖾ

Distinguished Cats

Sugar, the cat who walked 1,500 miles from California to Oklahoma, USA, in order to rejoin her family

Pepper, the motion picture cat, who starred alongside Charlie Chaplin

Wilberforce, the cat who lived in Downing Street from 1973-1988, through the rule of four prime ministers

Mourka, the cat of Stalingrad, who during World War II delivered vital messages from Russian scouts about enemy gun emplacements

Towzer, a champion ratter who killed 28,899 rats over 24 years while employed at the Glen Turret distillery on Tayside, Scotland

Snowball, the cat who helped lay cable for the Grand-Coulee Dam in Washington state, USA, by dragging a cable through bent piping

Fat Albert, the official blood donor for the cats of New Jersey, USA

Simon, the captain's cat, who was given the Dickin Medal in 1949 for bravery in protecting food supplies on the HMS Amethyst

Scarlett, the cat who ran into a burning house in New York five times to save her litter of kittens

Mike, the British Museum cat, who greeted visitors there for more than nineteen years

27

About 50 million years ago, the first ancestor of the cat appeared: the weasel-like Miacid.

In 500 BC, Persian soldiers carried cats into battle to protect themselves from the Egyptians, who were loath to harm the sacred animal.

At the turn of the 19th century, 300,000 mummified cats were unearthed in Beni Hasan, Egypt. Most were sent to England to be used as fertilizer.

HISTORICAL

Bastet, the Ancient Egyptian goddess of life, maternity and happiness, was also known as Pasht, from which "puss" is possibly derived.

Ancient Egyptians shaved off their eyebrows to mourn the death of a cat.

The Japanese revered cats for protecting their precious silkworms from mice. The cat statues at Gokoku-ji temple in Tokyo raise their paws for good luck.

Ancient Romans made sure to nod respectfully to passing cats for fear of being cursed with the "evil eye".

In the Middle Ages, people believed that witches could change into feline form – but only nine times.

In the 16th century, Prussian soldiers used "fire-cats", explosives strapped to their backs, to spread fire in enemy quarters.

ODDMENTS

St Agatha and St Gertrude are among several saints who are associated with cats. St Jerome is always depicted with his tame lion.

Dick Whittington's cat may not have been a cat at all, but the cat-boat that carried the coal that made the man's fortune.

Despite the fear and superstition surrounding the cat in the Middle Ages, its image was frequently featured in church carvings.

In medieval times, the herb rue was tied beneath the wings of chicks to repel hungry cats.

Up until the 18th century, a cat was often walled up in a newly built house to keep the devil – and the rats – away.

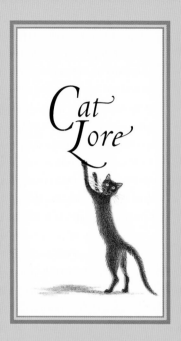

Cat Lore

*A bashful cat makes
a proud mouse.*

❖

*The cat with a straw tail
keeps away from fire.*

*Don't let the cat
out of the bag.*

❖

*It's raining
cats and dogs.*

*The dog wakes three times
to watch over its master;
The cat wakes three times
to strangle him.*

*When the cats go off,
the mice go dancing.*

❖

*Gloved cats catch
no mice.*

*A scalded cat
dreads cold water.*

❖

*He's as honest as the cat
when the meat's out of reach.*

*A dab of lard
cures all, even
the cat's boil.*

❖

*Rub a cat's paw
with butter, and
it will not stray.*

❖

*She that denies
the cat skimmed
milk must give
the mouse cream.*

✻

*Kiss the black cat,
t'will make ye fat;
Kiss the white one,
t'will make ye lean.*

✻

*Whenever the cat
of the house is black,
the lasses of lovers
will have no lack.*

✻

*A ship's cat that's black
brings bad luck;
a tortoiseshell cat
brings good.*

✻

*There'll be no playing
with straw
before an old cat.*

✻

*A halfpenny cat
may look at a king.*
✻
*Curiosity
killed the cat.*

*A cat will never drown
if it can see the shore.*
✻
*There's more than one
way to skin a cat.*

*There's not room
to swing a cat.*
✻
*The cat sees through
shut lids.*

Hungry Cats

JACK SPRAT
Had a cat,
It had but one ear;
It went to buy butter
When butter was dear.

RAT A TAT TAT who is that?
Only grandma's pussy cat.
What do you want?
A pint of milk.
Where's your money?
In my pocket.
Where's your pocket?
I forgot it.
Oh, you silly pussy cat!

PUSSY AT THE FIRESIDE suppin' up brose,
Down came a cinder and burned pussy's nose.
Oh, said pussy, that's no fair.
Well, said the cinder, you shouldn't be there.

HIE, HIE, SAYS ANTHONY,

Puss is in the pantry,
Gnawing, gnawing,
A mutton, mutton bone;
See how she tumbles it,
See how she mumbles it,
See how she tosses
The mutton, mutton bone.

SING, SING,

What shall I sing?
The cat's run away
With the pudding string!

Do, do,
What shall I do?
The cat's run away
With the pudding, too!

RINDLE, RANDLE,

Light the candle,
The cat's among the pies;
No matter for that,
The cat'll get fat,
And I'm too lazy to rise.

From The Kitten
and Falling Leaves

—But the Kitten, how she starts,

Crouches, stretches, paws and darts!

With a tiger-leap half-way

Now she meets the coming prey,

Lets it go as fast, and then

Has it in her power again.

WILLIAM WORDSWORTH

35

THE LION

The Lion, the Lion, he dwells in the waste,
He has a big head and a very small waist;
But his shoulders are stark,
and his jaws they are grim,
And a good little child
will not play with
him.

THE TIGER

The Tiger on the other hand, is kittenish and mild,

He makes a pretty playfellow for any little child;

And mothers of large families

    (who claim to common sense)

Will find a Tiger well repays

    the trouble and expense.

HILAIRE BELLOC

NICOLA BAYLEY is one of this country's best-loved artists, and particularly well-known for her exquisite pictures of cats. A great fan of all things feline, she says, "I've had cats all my life and collect *everything* to do with them – even their whiskers when they fall out! I've put pictures of my cats into almost every book I've ever done, and now, in **The Curious Cat**, I've made a book that celebrates *all* cats."

ISBN 0-7445-8939-8 (pb)

ISBN 0-7445-2353-2 (pb)

Nicola has illustrated many acclaimed picture books for children, including *All for the Newborn Baby*, *The Necessary Cat*, *Katje the Windmill Cat* and *The Mousehole Cat*, which was Winner of the Illustrated Children's Book of the Year in the British Book Awards, Commended for the Kate Greenaway Medal and shortlisted for both the Smarties Book Prize and the Children's Book Award. She lives in London with her family and, of course, her cats – Pansy and Tikki.